Sunbonn Sue

Once Upon a Posy™

Designs by Pearl Louise Krush

HOUSE of
WHITE
BIRCHES

PUBLISHERS
SINCE 1947

Tea Time Collection,
page 23

Table of Contents

Kitchen Collection, **page 39**

Porch Collection,
page 4

Chocolate & Cherries
Collection, **page 13**

Garden Collection,
page 28

Meet the Designer

I simply love to design projects that make people smile. Even as a small child, I enjoyed making things out of paper, clay and fabric.

As a young mother of three sons and the wife of a very busy husband, I wanted to make a little extra money for all of the extras every family needs. One of the earliest businesses I created was a "Barbie® Doll Party." I would have my friends and other moms have a Barbie Party, and I would show a collection of doll clothes that I had designed. They would order what they wanted, and I would then deliver and charge for the wardrobes that had been ordered. It was a great learning experience.

In 1989, I started the Pearl Louise Designs pattern company and started showing my designs at the International Quilt Market. When my local quilt shop closed, I decided to open The Thimble Cottage Quilt Shop as I needed quilt-shop fabrics to make my designs. The quilt shop and my home are in Rapid City, S.D., just a few miles from Mount Rushmore. During the summer months, we are very busy with visitors from around the world, and I truly enjoy meeting all of them. Over the years the shop has evolved into a place where customers can come and enjoy our collection of fabrics, classes and clubs that we offer, as well as our Web store, www.thimblecottage.com. I began designing fabric for the Troy Corp. several years ago and have found it very interesting and challenging. Most of my designs are whimsical winter and baby designs, but now I'm venturing into designing a home-decor collection, which should be tons of fun.

My husband, Fred, and I enjoy fishing in the summer months. We have two dogs, Bella and Kate, and Telly the bird (Bella goes to the shop every day.) My sons are grown, and we now have two wonderful daughters-in-law and three charming grandchildren.

One of my very favorite sayings has always been "Happiness Is Homemade."

Enjoy!

Pearl Louise Krush

Porch Collection

Enjoy a moment of rest and relax with Sunbonnet Sue and Overall Bill in floral designs for the porch or sunroom.

Project Note

Fabrics used in the projects in the Porch Collection are 1930s reproduction prints. Select fabric colors as desired, using sample projects as guides for fabric placement in the appliqué projects.

Project Specifications

Skill Level: Beginner
Quilt Size: 66" x 66"
Pillow Size: 16" x 16"
Block Sizes: 8" x 8" and 5" x 5"
Number of Blocks: 12 and 4

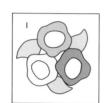

Small Flower
5" x 5" Block
Make 4

Overall Bill
8" x 8" Block
Make 2 & 2 reversed

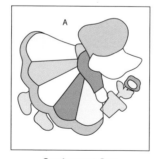

Sunbonnet Sue
8" x 8" Block
Make 2 & 2 reversed

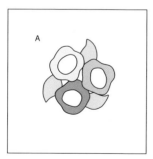

Large Flower
8" x 8" Block
Make 2

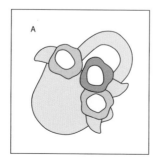

Flower Basket
8" x 8" Block
Make 2

Materials

- Scrap pink solid
- Fat eighth tan tonal
- Fat eighth green solid
- 8 fat quarters 1930s reproduction prints
- ¼ yard bubblegum pink solid
- ¾ yard each pink, blue and yellow 1930s reproduction prints
- 1⅛ yards muslin
- 2⅜ yards green 1930s reproduction print
- 2½ yards white tonal
- Backing 74" x 74"
- Batting 74" x 74" and 3 (18" x 18")
- Black and white all-purpose thread
- Quilting thread
- 1¾ yards 18"-wide fusible web
- Appliqué pressing sheet (optional)
- 3 (16" x 16") pillow forms
- Basic sewing tools and supplies

Instructions

Cutting

1. Cut three 8½" by fabric width strips white tonal; subcut strip into (12) 8½" A squares.

2. Cut two 14¾" by fabric width strips white tonal; subcut strips into three 14¾" squares, two 8⅝" x 8⅝" squares and four 5½" x 5½" I squares. Cut the 14¾" squares on both diagonals to make 12 E triangles and the 8⅝" squares in half on one diagonal to make four F triangles.

3. Cut six 2½" by fabric width H strips white tonal.

4. Cut five 2¾" by fabric width strips white tonal; subcut strips into six 12" K strips and six 16½" L strips.

5. Cut one 8½" x 21" strip from each of the eight fat quarters 1930s reproduction prints; subcut strips into two 8½" B squares each fabric.

6. Cut (11) 2½" x 21" strips total all 1930s reproduction prints for pillow binding.

7. Cut one 12" by fabric width strip each pink, blue and yellow 1930s reproduction prints; subcut strips

into two 16½" M pieces each fabric (six total) for pillow backings and two 6⅝" x 6⅝" squares each fabric. Cut the 6⅝" squares in half on one diagonal to make four J triangles each fabric; discard one triangle each fabric.

8. Cut (16) 2" by fabric width strips green print; subcut strips into (64) 8½" C strips.

9. Cut (11) 2" by fabric width G strips green print.

10. Cut one 6⅝" by fabric width strip green print; subcut strip into two 6⅝" squares. Cut each square in half on one diagonal to make four J triangles; discard one.

11. Cut seven 2½" by fabric width strips green print for quilt binding.

12. Cut two 18" by fabric width strips muslin; subcut strips into three 18" squares for pillow linings.

13. Cut two 2" by fabric width strips bubblegum pink solid; subcut strips into (40) 2" D squares.

14. Prepare templates for N and O pieces using patterns given; cut as directed on each piece.

15. Trace individual appliqué shapes as directed for number to cut onto the paper side of the fusible web; cut out shapes, leaving a ½" margin around each one. *Note: Trace and cut out two and two reversed apron shapes and set aside.*

16. Fuse shapes to the wrong side of fabrics as directed on patterns for color and number to cut; cut out shapes on traced lines. Remove paper backing.

Completing the Appliqué

1. Select and join three O pieces with one each N and NR pieces to make a pieced apron, referring to Figure 1. Repeat to make four pieced aprons.

Figure 1

2. Fuse the fusible web apron shapes cut in step 15 of Cutting instructions to the wrong side of each pieced apron. Trim the pieced apron even with the edges of the fusible web piece. Remove paper backing.

3. Fold and crease the A squares from corner to corner on both diagonals to find the diagonal center. Fold and crease the I squares horizontally and vertically to find the centers.

4. Center and fuse the appliqué motifs on the A and I squares in numerical order, referring to the patterns and block drawings for positioning. *Note: Using an appliqué pressing sheet to fuse the motif together before fusing to A or I helps make this process more accurate.*

5. Using black thread and a machine blanket stitch, stitch around each fused shape; set aside.

Completing the Quilt

1. Arrange and join the A and B squares in diagonal block rows with the C strips as shown in Figure 2; press seams toward C strips.

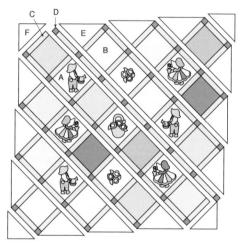

Figure 2

2. Arrange and join the remaining C strips with the D squares to make sashing rows, again referring to Figure 2; press seams toward C strips.

3. Join the block rows with the sashing rows and E and F triangles, again referring to Figure 2 to complete the pieced center; press seams toward sashing rows.

4. Join the G strips on short ends to make one long strip; press seams open. Subcut strip into eight 56½" G strips.

5. Repeat step 4 with H strips to cut four 56½" H strips.

6. Sew an H strip between two G strips along length to make a G-H strip; press seams toward G strips. Repeat to make four G-H strips.

7. Sew a G-H strip to opposite sides of the pieced center; press seams toward G-H strips.

8. Sew a Small Flower block to each end of each remaining G-H strip; press seams toward G-H strips.

9. Sew a G-H/Small Flower strip to the top and bottom of the pieced center to complete the top; press seams toward G-H/Small Flower strips.

10. Sandwich the 74" x 74" square batting between the same-size backing and the completed top; pin or baste layers together to hold flat.

11. Quilt as desired by hand or machine.

12. When quilting is complete, trim edges even and remove pins or basting.

13. Join the green print binding strips on short ends with diagonal seams to make one long strip as shown in Figure 3; trim seams to ¼" and press open.

Figure 3

14. Fold the binding strip in half with wrong sides together along length; press.

15. Stitch binding to the quilted top with raw edges even, mitering corners and overlapping at the beginning and end.

16. Turn the binding to the back side; hand- or machine-stitch in place to finish.

Completing the Pillows

1. Select one J triangle of each color; sew one to each side of the remaining appliquéd blocks, referring to the Placement Diagrams for color positioning suggestions; press seams toward J triangles.

2. Sew a K strip to opposite sides and L strips to the top and bottom of each bordered block to complete the pillow tops.

3. Sandwich an 18" batting square between an 18" muslin square and a completed pillow top; pin or baste layers together to hold flat.

4. Quilt as desired by hand or machine.

5. When quilting is complete, trim edges even and remove pins or basting.

6. Repeat steps 3–5 to complete three quilted pillow tops.

7. Turn under one 16½" edge of each M rectangle ¼"; press. Turn under ¼" again, press and stitch close to first fold to make hemmed edge.

8. Place two M rectangles wrong sides together with each quilted pillow top, overlapping edges of M as shown in Figure 4; pin in place. Baste overlapped edges to hold.

On Point Porch Quilt
Placement Diagram 66" x 66"

Figure 4

9. Join the 21"-long reproduction print binding strips on short ends with diagonal seams to make one long strip, again referring to Figure 3; trim seams to ¼" and press open.

10. Fold the binding strip in half with wrong sides together along length; press.

11. Stitch the binding strip to the edges of one pillow cover with raw edges even, mitering corners and overlapping at the beginning and end. Repeat with remaining pillow covers.

12. Turn the binding to the back side; hand- or machine-stitch in place.

13. Insert a pillow form in each pillow cover to finish. ❖

Sunbonnet Sue With Flower Pillow
Placement Diagram 16" x 16"

Flower Motif
Prepare 6—4 appliquéd to
I squares & 2 appliquéd to B squares
Cut pieces from fabrics in desired colors,
using green solid for leaves

House of White Birches, Berne, Indiana 46711 Clotilde.com

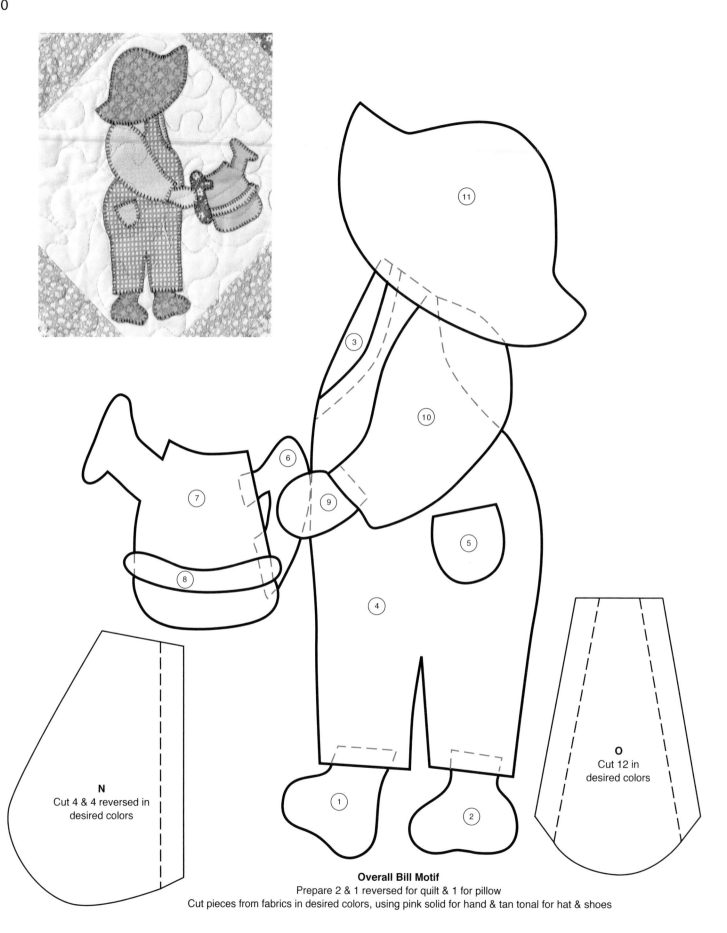

N
Cut 4 & 4 reversed in
desired colors

O
Cut 12 in
desired colors

Overall Bill Motif
Prepare 2 & 1 reversed for quilt & 1 for pillow
Cut pieces from fabrics in desired colors, using pink solid for hand & tan tonal for hat & shoes

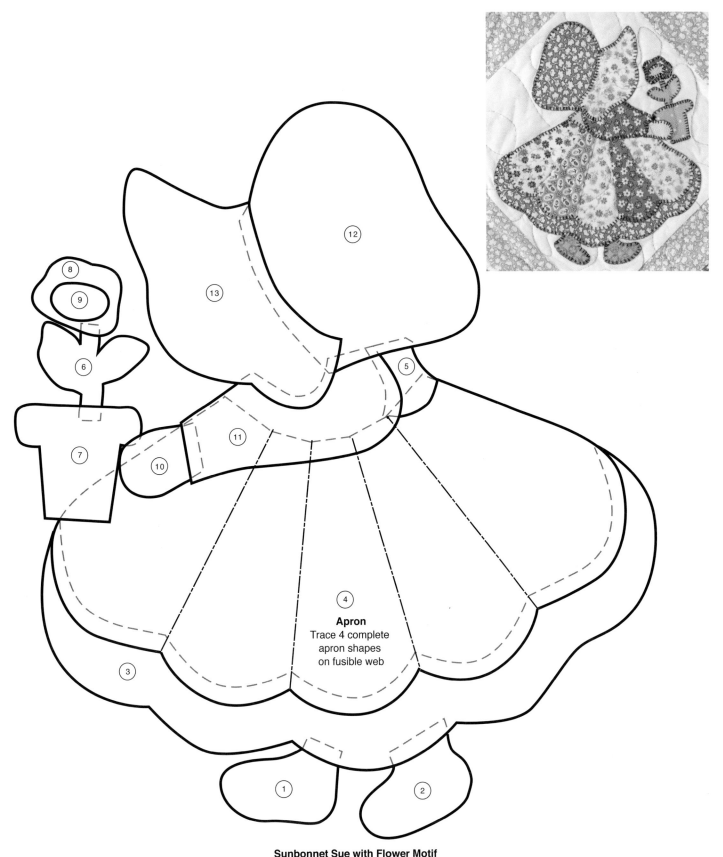

Sunbonnet Sue with Flower Motif
Prepare 1 & 2 reversed for quilt & 1 for pillow
Cut pieces from fabrics in desired colors, using pink solid for hand, tan tonal for flower pot & green solid for leaves

Apron
Trace 4 complete
apron shapes
on fusible web

House of White Birches, Berne, Indiana 46711   Clotilde.com

12

Flower Basket Motif
Prepare 1 for quilt & 1 for pillow
Cut pieces from fabrics in desired colors, using green tonal for leaves & tan tonal for basket

Chocolate & Cherries Collection

These designs will sweeten your mealtime with their bright colors. The table topper, casserole holder, pot holder and coasters in this collection will add cheer to your table.

Project Specifications
Skill Level: Beginner
Topper Size: 36" x 36"
Pot Holder Size: 8" x 8"
Coaster Size: 4" x 4"
Casserole Holder Size: 11" x 11" x 3½"
Block Size: 8" x 8"
Number of Blocks: 11

Materials
- Scrap pink solid
- ⅜ yard white tonal
- 1 fat quarter each green and 2 yellow prints
- ½ yard red check
- ⅞ yard white dot
- 1 yard brown mottled
- 2⅛ yards bubblegum pink print
- Backing 44" x 44"
- 2⅛ yards 44"-wide batting
- 10½" x 10½" square heat-resistant batting
- Neutral-color and black all-purpose thread
- Quilting thread
- ⅝ yard 18"-wide fusible web
- Appliqué pressing sheet (optional)
- 9½" x 9½" square foam board
- 3 (¾") brown buttons
- ¼ yard ¼"-wide black elastic
- Water-erasable marker or pencil
- Basic sewing tools and supplies

Overall Bill
8" x 8" Block
Make 2

Sunbonnet Sue
8" x 8" Block
Make 2

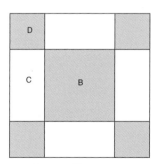

Uneven Nine-Patch
8" x 8" Block
Make 5

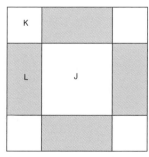

Reverse Uneven Nine-Patch
8" x 8" Block
Make 2

House of White Birches, Berne, Indiana 46711   Clotilde.com

Cutting Instructions

1. Cut one 8½" by fabric width strip white tonal; subcut strip into four 8½" A squares.

2. Cut three 4½" by fabric width strips white dot; subcut strips into (20) 2½" C rectangles, six 4½" J squares and eight 2½" x 2½" K squares.

3. Cut four 2½" x 28½" H strips white dot.

4. Cut eight 1½" x 28½" G strips bubblegum pink print.

5. Cut two 4½" by fabric width strips bubblegum pink print; subcut strips into eight 2½" L rectangles and nine 4½" B squares.

6. Cut two 2½" by fabric width strips bubblegum pink print; subcut strips into (20) 2½" D squares.

7. Cut one 14" by fabric width O-P strip bubblegum pink print.

8. Cut two 11½" by fabric width strips bubblegum pink print; subcut strips into three 11½" P squares and four 4" O strips.

9. Cut one 9¾" by fabric width strip bubblegum pink print; subcut strip into two 9¾" Q squares.

10. Cut one 14" by fabric width muslin O-P strip.

11. Cut one 8½" by fabric width strip brown mottled; subcut strip into (24) 1½" E strips.

12. Cut one 4½" by fabric width strip brown mottled; subcut strip into four 4½" I squares.

13. Cut one 2" by fabric width strip brown mottled; subcut strip into two 8½" M strips and two 11½" N strips.

14. Cut four 2¼" by fabric width strips red check for table topper binding.

15. Cut one 1½" by fabric width strip red check; subcut strip into (16) 1½" F squares.

16. Cut five 2¼" by fabric width strips brown mottled for binding for pot holder, casserole cover and coasters.

17. Cut the following from batting: one 14" x 42" for O and P pieces; one 11½" x 11½" for casserole cover lid; four 4½" x 4½" squares for coasters; and one 44" x 44" square for table topper.

18. Trace individual appliqué shapes as directed for number to cut onto the paper side of the fusible web; cut out shapes, leaving a ½" margin around each one.

19. Fuse shapes to the wrong side of fabrics as directed on patterns for color and number to cut for two each Sunbonnet Sue and Overall Bill motifs; cut out shapes on traced lines. Remove paper backing.

Completing the Appliqué

1. Fold and crease each A square on the diagonals to find the center as shown in Figure 1.

Figure 1

2. Center and fuse a Sunbonnet Sue motif in numerical order on the diagonal of two A squares; repeat with Overall Bill on the remaining two A squares. *Note: Using an appliqué pressing sheet to fuse the motif together before fusing to E helps make this process more accurate.*

3. Using black thread and a machine blanket stitch, stitch around each fused shape.

Completing the Uneven Nine-Patch Blocks

1. To make one Uneven Nine-Patch block, sew a B square between two C rectangles to make a B-C unit as shown in Figure 2; press seams toward B.

Figure 2

2. Sew C between two D squares to make a C-D unit; press seams toward D. Repeat to make two C-D units.

3. Sew a C-D unit to opposite sides of the B-C unit to complete one Uneven Nine-Patch block referring to the block drawing for positioning of units; press seams away from the B-C unit.

4. Repeat steps 1–3 to complete five Uneven Nine-Patch blocks.

Completing the Reverse Uneven Nine-Patch Blocks

1. To make one Reverse Uneven Nine-Patch block, sew a J square between two L rectangles to make a J-L unit as shown in Figure 3; press seams toward L.

Figure 3

2. Sew L between two K squares to make a K-L unit; press seams toward L. Repeat to make two K-L units.

3. Sew a K-L unit to opposite sides of the J-L unit to complete one Reverse Uneven Nine-Patch block referring to the block drawing for positioning of units; press seams away from the J-L unit.

4. Repeat steps 1–3 to complete two Reverse Uneven Nine-Patch blocks.

Completing the Pot Holder

1. Sandwich the 10½" x 10½" square heat-resistant batting between one Reverse Uneven Nine-Patch block and a P square; pin or baste layers together to hold.

2. Quilt as desired by hand or machine; remove pins or basting.

3. Trim batting and backing edges even with the pot-holder top.

4. Join the three brown mottled binding strips on short ends with diagonal seams to make one long strip as shown in Figure 4; trim seams to ¼" and press open.

Figure 4

5. Fold the strip in half along length with wrong sides together; press.

6. With raw edges even, pin the binding strip to the right side of the pot holder; stitch all around, mitering corners and overlapping at the beginning and end. Trim excess binding.

7. Turn binding to the back side; hand-stitch in place.

8. Cut a 5" length from the remaining end of the trimmed binding strip. Set aside remainder of strip for casserole cover and coasters.

9. Unfold the 5" strip and fold again along length with right sides together; stitch along long raw edge as shown in Figure 5.

Figure 5

10. Turn the stitched tube right side out and press flat with seam on the side; topstitch close to each long edge.

11. Fold each end of the strip ⅜" to the wrong side then fold the strip in half with the folded ends between to make a loop as shown in Figure 6.

Figure 6

12. Hand-stitch ends of loop in place on one corner of the back side of the pot holder to finish. ***Note:*** *If you want to hang your pot holder as shown in the photos on pages 14 and 16, hand-stitch one end of the strip to the back of the pot holder and use a snap to attach the other end.*

Pot Holder
Placement Diagram 8" x 8"

Completing the Table Topper

1. Arrange and join one each Sunbonnet Sue, Overall Bill and Uneven Nine-Patch block with four E strips to make an X row as shown in Figure 7; press seams toward E strips. Repeat to make two X rows.

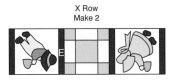

Figure 7

2. Join three Uneven Nine-Patch blocks with four E strips to make a Y row, referring to Figure 8; press seams toward E strips.

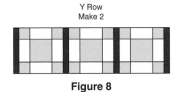

Figure 8

3. Join three E strips with four F squares to make a sashing row as shown in Figure 9; press seams toward F squares. Repeat to make four sashing rows.

Figure 9

4. Join the X and Y rows with the sashing rows, referring to the Placement Diagram; press seams toward sashing rows.

5. Sew an H strip between two G strips along length; press seams toward G strips. Repeat to make four G-H strips.

6. Sew a G-H strip to opposite sides of the pieced center; press seams toward G-H strips.

7. Sew an I square to each end of each remaining G-H strip; press seams toward the G-H strips.

8. Sew a G-H-I strip to the remaining sides of the pieced center to complete the pieced top; press seams toward G-H-I strips.

9. Sandwich the 44" x 44" batting square between the completed top and prepared backing piece; pin or baste layers together to hold flat.

10. Quilt as desired by hand or machine.

11. When quilting is complete, remove pins or basting and trim edges even.

12. Prepare binding using the four 2¼" red check strips, referring to steps 4 and 5 of Completing the Pot Holder. Pin and stitch the prepared binding to top side of the topper, matching raw edges, mitering corners and overlapping at the beginning and end.

13. Turn binding to the back side and hand- or machine-stitch in place to complete the table topper.

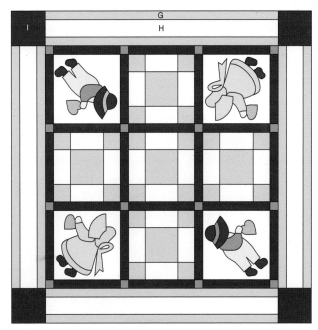

Table Topper
Placement Diagram 36" x 36"

Completing the Casserole Holder

1. Sew an M strip to two opposite sides and N strips to the remaining sides of the remaining Reverse Uneven Nine-Patch block as shown in Figure 10; press seams toward M and N strips.

Figure 10

2. Sandwich the 11½" x 11½" batting square between the bordered block and one P square; pin or baste layers to hold flat.

3. Quilt as desired; when quilting is complete, trim edges even and remove pins or basting.

4. Pin and stitch the prepared brown binding to top side of the block, matching raw edges, mitering corners and overlapping at the beginning and end; trim excess.

5. Turn binding to the back side and hand- or machine-stitch in place to complete the casserole holder lid; set aside.

6. Sandwich the 14" x 42" O-P batting rectangle between the same-size O-P bubblegum pink print and muslin rectangles; pin or baste layers together to hold flat.

7. Machine-quilt as desired; remove pins or basting when quilting is complete.

8. From the quilted rectangle, cut one 11½" x 11½" P square and four 4" x 11½" O strips.

9. Sew a quilted O strip right sides together to each side of the quilted P square, beginning and ending stitching ¼" from each end as shown in Figure 11; press seams toward P.

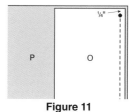

Figure 11

10. Join the ends of the O strips to make a square box, starting at the outside edge and stitching toward the inside edge, stopping stitching ¼" from the inside end as shown in Figure 12; press seams open.

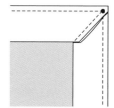

Figure 12

11. Repeat steps 9 and 10 with the unquilted O and P pieces.

12. Set the quilted O-P unit inside the unquilted O-P unit wrong sides together, aligning corners; pin to secure.

13. With raw edges even, pin the brown binding strip to the inside of the O-P unit; stitch all around, mitering corners and overlapping at the beginning and end. Trim excess binding.

14. Turn binding to the outside; hand-stitch in place.

15. Pinch the corners of the bound O-P bottom unit together and securely hand-stitch together at the top binding edge ½" from fold as shown in Figure 13.

Figure 13

16. Align one edge of the casserole holder lid with one edge of the O-P bottom unit and hand-stitch together at the edges of the binding as shown in Figure 14 to create the covered casserole holder.

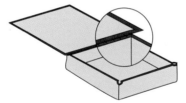

Figure 14

17. Center and sew a button on the remaining three sides 1" from the top edge of the binding.

18. Cut the ¼"-wide black elastic into three 2½" lengths; cut ends of each length at an angle to prevent raveling.

19. Fold each length of elastic in half to make a loop; center and securely hand-stitch an elastic loop ½" to the back side of the casserole cover.

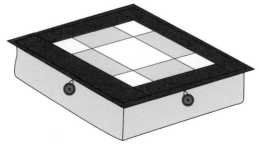

Casserole Holder
Placement Diagram 11" x 11" x 3½"

20. Place the Q squares right sides together; stitch around three sides. Turn right side out; press flat. Turn under open edge ¼"; press and stitch to hem.

21. Insert the 9½" x 9½" foam board square inside the pocket. Place the pocket into the bottom of the casserole holder to finish.

22. Pull elastic loops around buttons to hold closed when in use.

Completing the Coasters

1. Sandwich the 4½" x 4½" batting squares between the B and J squares; quilt as desired.

2. Bind the edges of each quilted B/J square as for the pot holder to complete the four coasters. ❖

Coaster
Placement Diagram 4" x 4"

yellow print #2

8

green print

9

pink solid

5

yellow print #2

7

bubblegum pink

4

green print

10

green print

6

yellow print #2

3

brown mottled

2

brown mottled

1

Sunbonnet Sue Motif
Prepare 2 for table topper
Cut pieces from fabrics in indicated colors

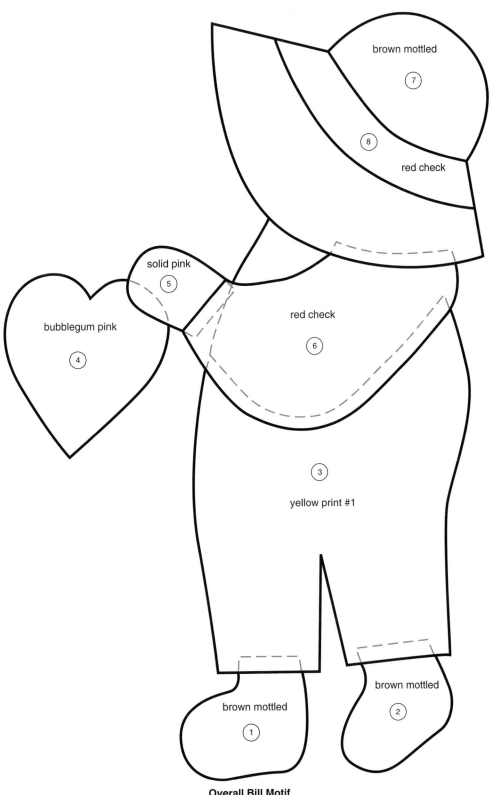

brown mottled

7

8

red check

solid pink

5

red check

bubblegum pink

6

4

3

yellow print #1

brown mottled

brown mottled

1

2

Overall Bill Motif
Prepare 2 for table topper
Cut pieces from fabrics in indicated colors

Tea Time Collection

It's a tea party with Sunbonnet Sue and this cheerful tea cozy and table runner set.

Project Notes

Use the Flower pattern given with the Garden Collection on page 34 for the tea cozy and runner, referring to the Placement Diagram and sample photo for color selection and placement.

The fabrics used in the piecing and appliqué on the runner and tea cozy are 1930s reproduction prints in the typical colors of that era.

Project Specifications

Skill Level: Beginner
Runner Size: 47⅜" x 14⅛"
Tea Cozy Size: 8" x 8"
Block Size: 10" x 10"
Number of Blocks: 3

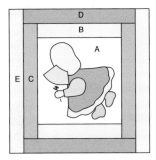

Sunbonnet Log Cabin
10" x 10" Block
Make 2

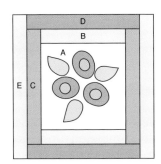

Floral Log Cabin
10" x 10" Block
Make 1

Materials

- Scraps tan tonal and pink solid
- Fat eighth green print
- Fat eighth pink check
- 1 fat quarter each white, blue and purple prints
- ⅜ yard cream/blue floral
- ⅜ yard lavender print
- ⅞ yard cream tonal
- Backing 20" x 54"
- Batting 20" x 54" for runner and (2) 8½" x 8½" for tea cozy
- Neutral-color all-purpose thread
- Pastel variegated thread

- Quilting thread
- Purple and green embroidery floss
- 1 yard 18"-wide fusible web
- Appliqué pressing sheet (optional)
- 1 yard ⅛"-wide lavender ribbon
- Large safety pin
- Basic sewing tools and supplies

Cutting Instructions

1. Cut one 15⅜" by fabric width strip cream tonal; subcut strip into one 15⅜" square, three 6½" x 6½" A squares and two each 2" x 12" G and 2" x 13" H strips. Cut the 15⅜" square on both diagonals to make four F triangles.

2. Cut one 8½" by fabric width strip cream tonal; subcut strip into two 8½" I squares.

3. Cut one 1½" by fabric width strip cream/blue floral; subcut strip into six 6½" B strips.

4. Cut three 2¼" by fabric width strips cream/blue floral for binding.

5. Cut three 1½" x 21" strips blue print; subcut strips into six 8½" C strips.

6. Cut three 1½" x 21" strips purple print; subcut strips into six 8½" D strips.

7. Cut three 1½" x 21" strips white print; subcut strips into six 10½" E strips.

8. Cut one 8½" by fabric width strip lavender print; subcut strip into two 8½" tea-cozy lining squares and four 2" x 8½" J strips.

9. Trace individual appliqué shapes for two each Sunbonnet Sue and Flower motifs as directed for number to cut onto the paper side of the fusible web; cut out shapes, leaving a ½" margin around each one.

10. Fuse shapes to the wrong side of fabrics as directed on patterns for color and number to cut; cut out shapes on traced lines. Remove paper backing.

House of White Birches, Berne, Indiana 46711   Clotilde.com

Completing the Appliqué

1. Fold and crease each A and one I square horizontally and vertically to find the center.

2. Center and fuse a Sunbonnet Sue motif on two A squares in numerical order, marking the flower stitching lines in hand from motif. *Note: Using an appliqué pressing sheet to fuse the motif together before fusing to A helps make this process more accurate.*

3. Center and fuse a Flower motif on one A and one I square in numerical order.

4. Using pastel variegated thread and a machine blanket stitch, stitch around each fused shape.

5. Using 3 strands purple embroidery floss and a chain stitch, sew around the outside edges of the flower shapes on each square.

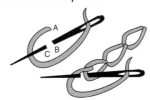

Chain Stitch

6. Repeat step 5 with 1 strand purple embroidery floss and six Lazy Daisy stitches to make flowers and 1 strand green embroidery floss and a stem stitch to make the stem on each Sunbonnet Sue square.

Lazy Daisy Stitch

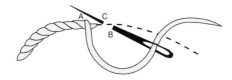

Stem Stitch

Completing the Log Cabin Blocks

1. To complete an appliquéd Log Cabin block, select one appliquéd A square; sew a B strip to opposite sides as shown in Figure 1. Press seams toward B strips.

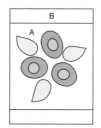

Figure 1

2. Continue adding strips to A in alphabetical order, referring to the block drawings; press seams toward strips as added to complete one block.

3. Repeat steps 1 and 2 to complete one Floral Log Cabin and two Sunbonnet Log Cabin blocks, referring to the block drawing.

Completing the Runner

1. Arrange and join the Floral Log Cabin block with the Sunbonnet Sue Log Cabin blocks and F triangles in diagonal rows, referring to Figure 2; press seams toward F triangles.

Figure 2

2. Stitch the F block rows together, again referring to Figure 2. Press seams in one direction.

3. Sew G and H strips to the remaining sides of the Log Cabin blocks on each end, referring to Figure 3; press seams toward G and H strips. Trim the extended ends of G and H even with the edges of the F triangles to complete the runner top, again referring to Figure 3.

Figure 3

4. Sandwich the 20" x 54" piece of batting between the completed runner top and prepared backing piece; pin or baste layers together to hold flat.

5. Quilt as desired by hand or machine. When quilting is complete, remove pins or basting and trim edges even.

6. Join the binding strips on short ends with a diagonal seam as shown in Figure 4; trim seam and press open.

Figure 4

7. Fold the binding strip in half with wrong sides together along length; press.

(top right) 25

8. Pin and stitch binding to back side of the runner, matching raw edges, mitering corners and overlapping at the beginning and end.

9. Turn binding to the front side and machine-stitch in place close to the folded edge to finish the runner.

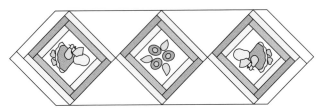

Table Runner
Placement Diagram 47³/₈" x 14¹/₈"

Completing the Tea Cozy

1. Layer the appliquéd I square and a tea cozy lining square right sides together on one 8½" x 8½" batting square.

2. Stitch all around, leaving a 3" opening on the bottom edge; trim batting close to seam. Turn right side out through the opening.

3. Press edges flat. Turn edges of opening to the inside; hand-stitch opening closed.

4. Press ¼" to the wrong side on each long edge of each J strip. Repeat on each short end; stitch each short end to form hem.

5. Pin a pressed J strip on the stitched I unit 1" down from the top and 1" up from the bottom edge as shown in Figure 5; topstitch in place ⅛" from edge on each long side of each strip, again referring to Figure 5, to make casings.

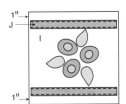

Figure 5

6. Repeat steps 1–5 with remaining I square, lining square and J strips to complete the tea-cozy back.

7. Cut the length of ribbon in half to make two equal lengths.

House of White Birches, Berne, Indiana 46711   Clotilde.com

8. Using a large safety pin on the end of each length, thread a piece of ribbon through both the top and bottom casings on the front and back to join as shown in Figure 6; tie ends into a bow to keep from escaping the casings.

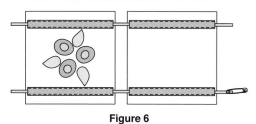

Figure 6

9. To use, place tea cozy over a teapot, pull the ribbon ends to gather and tie to hold snug to the teapot. ❖

Tea Cozy
Placement Diagram 8" x 8"

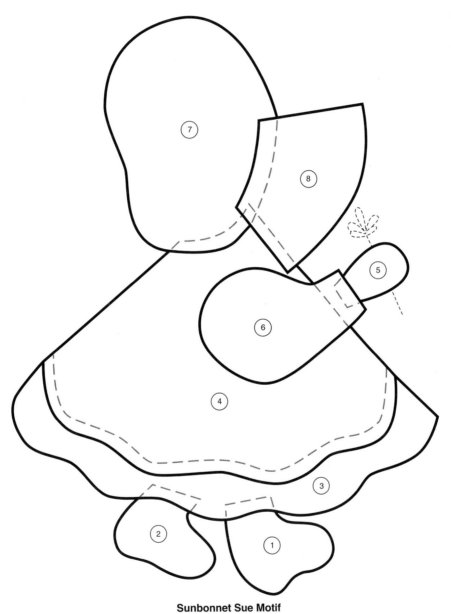

Sunbonnet Sue Motif
Prepare 2 for table runner
Cut pieces from fabrics in desired colors, using tan tonal for shoes & pink solid for hand

House of White Birches, Berne, Indiana 46711   Clotilde.com

Garden Collection

Sunbonnet Sue loves to go outside in garden-themed designs. Let the denim shirt, clothespin bag and garden tote make chore time a fun time.

Project Note

Fabrics used in the projects in the Garden Collection are 1930s reproduction prints. Select fabric colors as desired, using sample projects as guides for fabric placement in the appliqué projects.

Project Specifications

Skill Level: Beginner
Shirt Size: Size varies
Clothespin Holder Size: Approximately 7½" x 14"
Tote Size: 14" x 12" x 3"

Materials

- Scraps tan tonal and pink solid
- Fat eighths or scraps of 14 different reproduction prints
- Fat eighth pink check
- Fat eighth yellow tonal
- ¼ yard white tonal
- ½ yard muslin
- ½ yard yellow print
- ⅝ yard pink print
- 1 yard green print
- 1¼ yards 44"-wide batting
- Black and white all-purpose thread
- Pastel variegated thread
- ½ yard 18"-wide fusible web
- Appliqué pressing sheet (optional)
- Denim shirt
- 2 each 1⅛" yellow and dark purple buttons
- 1 yard ⅛"-wide yellow ribbon
- Water-erasable marker or pencil
- Large safety pin
- Basic sewing tools and supplies

Cutting Instructions

1. Cut (14) 2½" x 12½" A strips and (14) 2½" x 5½" B strips from the reproduction prints.

2. Cut one 18" by fabric width strip green print.

3. Cut one 7½" by fabric width strip green print; subcut strip into two 16½" C rectangles.

4. Cut two 2½" by fabric width strips green print for binding.

5. Cut one 4½" by fabric width strip white tonal; subcut strip into one 5½" F rectangle. Set aside remainder of strip to cut pocket scallop.

6. Cut one 12½" by fabric width strip pink print; subcut strip into two 14½" lining pieces.

7. Cut one 3½" by fabric width strip pink print; subcut strip into one 14½" bottom and two 12½" side lining strips.

8. Cut one 20" x 44", two 14½" x 16½" and two 7½" x 16½" batting rectangles.

9. Cut one 12½" by fabric width strip yellow print; subcut strip into one 12½" H square and two 6½" G rectangles for clothespin holder.

10. Cut one 2" x 21" strip yellow tonal for clothespin holder hanging loop.

11. Prepare templates for clothespin-holder yoke, yo-yo circle and pocket piece using patterns given; cut as directed on each piece.

12. Trace individual appliqué shapes (including pocket scallop) as directed for number to cut onto the paper side of the fusible web; cut out shapes, leaving a ½" margin around each one.

13. Fuse shapes to the wrong side of fabrics as directed on patterns for color and number to cut; cut out shapes on traced lines. Remove paper backing.

Completing the Appliqué

1. Fold and crease the F rectangle horizontally and vertically to find the center.

2. Align grass shape of the medium Sunbonnet Sue motif with one 4½" edge of F; fuse in place.

3. Center and fuse the remaining pieces of the motif on F in numerical order. *Note: Using an appliqué pressing sheet to fuse the motif together before fusing to F helps make this process more accurate.*

4. Using black thread and a machine blanket stitch, stitch around each fused shape; set aside.

5. Repeat steps 2 and 3 with the small Sunbonnet Sue motif on the clothespin-holder yoke piece, referring to the Placement Diagram for positioning. Stitch in place using pastel variegated thread as in step 4.

6. Center and fuse the large Sunbonnet Sue motif above the chest pocket on the denim shirt, referring to the Placement Diagram for positioning.

7. Stitch pieces in place using pastel variegated thread as in step 4.

8. Fuse the scallop piece on the top edge of one pink check pocket.

9. Using a water-erasable marker or pencil, trace the flower motif on one pink pocket piece. Arrange and fuse the flower and leaf shapes on the pocket using marked lines as guides.

10. Stitch scallop curved edges and flower motif in place using pastel variegated thread as in step 4.

Completing the Tote

1. Sandwich the 20" x 44" piece of batting between the ½ yard muslin and the 18" by fabric width piece green print; quilt as desired. Trim edges even.

2. Cut two 3½" x 12½" D tote side panels, one 3½" x 14½" E bottom panel and two 5" x 24" strap strips from the quilted panel.

3. Join seven different A strips along long edges to make an A panel as shown in Figure 1; press seams in one direction. Repeat to make two A panels.

Figure 1

4. Repeat step 3 with B strips to make two B panels, again referring to Figure 1.

5. Center and baste the appliquéd F rectangle on one B panel, aligning top and bottom edges as shown in Figure 2.

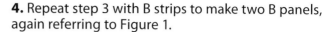

Figure 2

6. Using black thread and a machine blanket stitch, stitch F side edges in place; set aside.

7. Sandwich a 7½" x 16½" batting rectangle between a C rectangle and one B panel; quilt as desired. When quilting is complete trim edges even. Repeat with second panel.

8. Fold one 2½" by fabric width green print binding strip with wrong sides together along length; press. Cut the folded strip into two 16½" lengths for binding.

9. Pin and stitch one binding strip to the top edge of the front side of each B panel, matching raw edges. Turn the binding strips to the back side; hand-stitch in place to finish B pockets.

10. Place an A panel right side up on a 14½" x 16½" batting rectangle; quilt as desired. When quilting is complete, trim batting even with the edge of the A panel. Repeat for second A panel.

11. Layer the appliquéd B panel right side up on an A panel matching raw edges of B with raw edges of A as shown in Figure 3; machine baste in place to hold. Repeat with the back B panel.

Figure 3

12. Lay out the tote sections as shown in Figure 4.

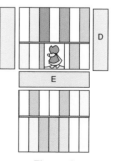

Figure 4

13. With right sides together, sew a quilted D piece to one end of the basted A/B front, stopping ¼" from the bottom corner; press seam to one side. Repeat with a second D panel on the opposite end.

14. Add the back A/B panel to join the front, back and side panels as shown in Figure 5, stopping stitching ¼" from the bottom corners as in step 13; press seams to one side.

Figure 5

15. With right sides together, sew bottom E panel to the bottom edge of the first D panel, stopping stitching ¼" from each corner, and leaving the needle down, rotate and sew the bottom E panel to the bottom of the front panel; continue in this fashion until the bottom panel has been inserted all around.

16. Turn the stitched tote right side out.

17. Repeat steps 12–16 with the pink print lining pieces.

18. Insert the stitched lining inside the tote with the wrong side of the lining against the wrong side of the tote shell; pin top raw edges together, matching seams of lining to seams of tote. Machine-baste around top edge to hold.

19. Fold a quilted 5" x 24" strap strip in half with right sides together along length; stitch with a ⅜" seam. Center seam and press open. Trim seam allowance to ⅛". Turn right side out and press flat with seam centered. Topstitch close to the seam and ¼" from each outside edge to complete one strap strip as shown in Figure 6. Repeat with the remaining strap strip.

Figure 6   **Figure 7**

20. Pin one end of a strap to the lining side on the front of the tote 1½" in from the side seam and the remaining end to the lining side on the back of the tote 1½" from the side seam as shown in Figure 7. Repeat with the second strap.

21. Prepare and apply second 2½" by fabric width binding strip to the top edge of the lining side of the tote as in step 8, overlapping at the beginning and end. Turn entire binding to the front of the tote. Hand-stitch binding in place. *Note: There will be no binding showing on the lining side.*

22. Pleat the top edge of each D side panel, matching side seams as shown in Figure 8; hand-stitch 1½" from side seams and 2" down from top edge through all layers to hold.

Figure 8

23. Sew a 1⅛" dark purple button on one side of the pleat and through a yellow button on the other side; repeat on the other end to finish tote.

Tote
Placement Diagram
14" x 12" x 3"

Completing the Denim Shirt

1. Pin the pocket lining piece right sides together with the appliquéd pocket; stitch all around, leaving a 3" opening on the bottom. Clip into seam every ¼" on the curved sides.

2. Turn right side out through opening; press opening edges to the inside and edges of pocket flat (Figure 9).

Figure 9

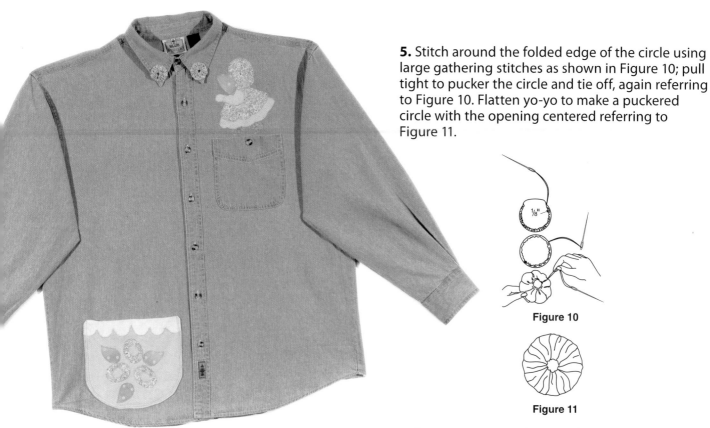

5. Stitch around the folded edge of the circle using large gathering stitches as shown in Figure 10; pull tight to pucker the circle and tie off, again referring to Figure 10. Flatten yo-yo to make a puckered circle with the opening centered referring to Figure 11.

Figure 10

Figure 11

6. Repeat steps 4 and 5 to make a second yo-yo.

7. Pin and stitch a yo-yo in place on each collar point, stitching all around the outside of each yo-yo to finish the Denim Shirt.

Completing the Clothespin Holder

1. Place the appliquéd and plain yoke pieces right side up on the yoke batting pieces; machine-baste around edges to hold layers together.

2. Place the two yoke/batting pieces right sides together; stitch around curved sides. Trim batting close to stitching; clip into curved seams close to stitching.

3. Turn the stitched yoke section right side out; press flat.

4. Fold one long edge of each G piece to the wrong side ¼" and press. Repeat and stitch to hem one long edge. Repeat with the second G piece.

5. Matching same-length raw edges, stitch each G to H to complete a G-H panel as shown in Figure 12.

3. Pin and stitch the pocket in place approximately 1" from bottom and 3" from side edges of the denim shirt, leaving top edge open; sew a second line of stitching ⅛" from the first line to finish the pocket.

4. Fold the edge of a yo-yo circle ⅛" to the wrong side. Thread a needle with 2 strands of thread; knot the end.

Denim Shirt
Placement Diagram
Size Varies

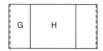

Figure 12

6. Overlap the hemmed edges ¾" at the top and bottom edges and baste to hold as shown in Figure 13.

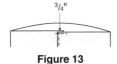

Figure 13

7. Fold the bottom edge under ¼"; press. Fold to the wrong side 1"; stitch in place, leaving a 1" opening at the end in which to insert the ribbon.

8. Pin the large safety pin to one end of the ribbon; insert in opening and push the pin/ribbon around the hemmed area until it comes out the same opening. Pull the ribbon taut to tightly gather the bottom edge and tie in a square knot to secure. Trim ribbon ends to 1" long; tuck inside.

9. Sew two rows of large machine gathering stitches ¼" and ⅜" from the top edge of the bag as shown in Figure 14. Pull the bobbin threads to make the gathered edge 7½" long.

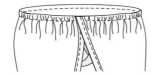

Figure 14

10. Center the overlapped center top edge of bag right sides together on the appliquéd yoke piece and adjust the remainder of the gathered edge to fit around the stitched yoke unit matching side seams, as shown in Figure 15; machine-baste in place. Check the stitching for even gathering and pleated areas; if satisfied with stitching, sew over basting stitches. Turn right side out.

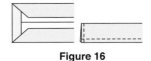

Figure 15

11. Fold each short end of the 2" x 21" loop strip to the wrong side ¼"; press. Fold strip in half wrong sides together lengthwise, press, then unfold. Fold each long raw edge of the strip to the pressed center with wrong sides together as shown in Figure 16; press.

Figure 16

12. Fold the strip in half along length, pressing and then stitching edges together to make the loop strip, again referring to Figure 16.

13. Fold the strip length in half and hand-stitch in place at the top center of the yoke section to securely hold in place. Tie strip in a bow at top, leaving a loop, and hang in desired location; fill with clothespins to use. ❖

Clothespin Holder
Placement Diagram
Approximately 7½" x 14"

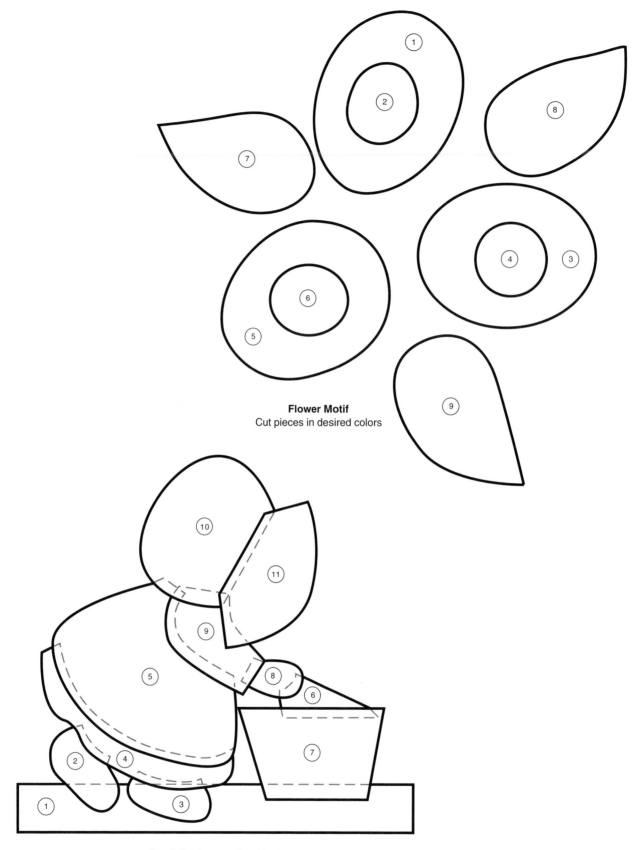

Flower Motif
Cut pieces in desired colors

Small Sunbonnet Sue Motif
Prepare 1 for clothespin holder
Cut pieces from fabrics in desired colors, using
tan tonal for shoes & pink solid for hand

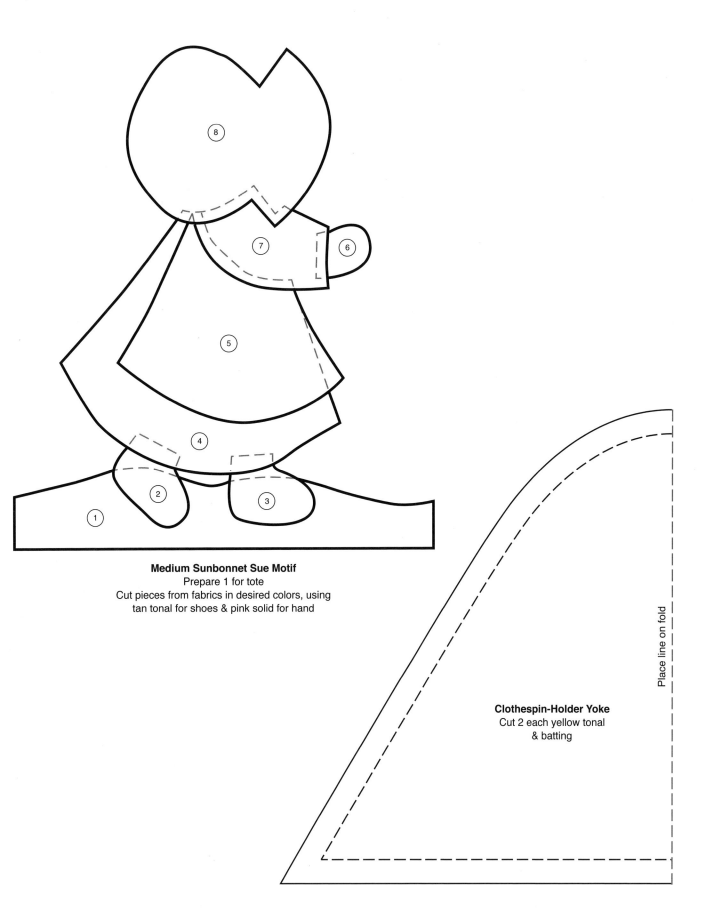

Medium Sunbonnet Sue Motif
Prepare 1 for tote
Cut pieces from fabrics in desired colors, using
tan tonal for shoes & pink solid for hand

Clothespin-Holder Yoke
Cut 2 each yellow tonal
& batting

Place line on fold

House of White Birches, Berne, Indiana 46711   Clotilde.com

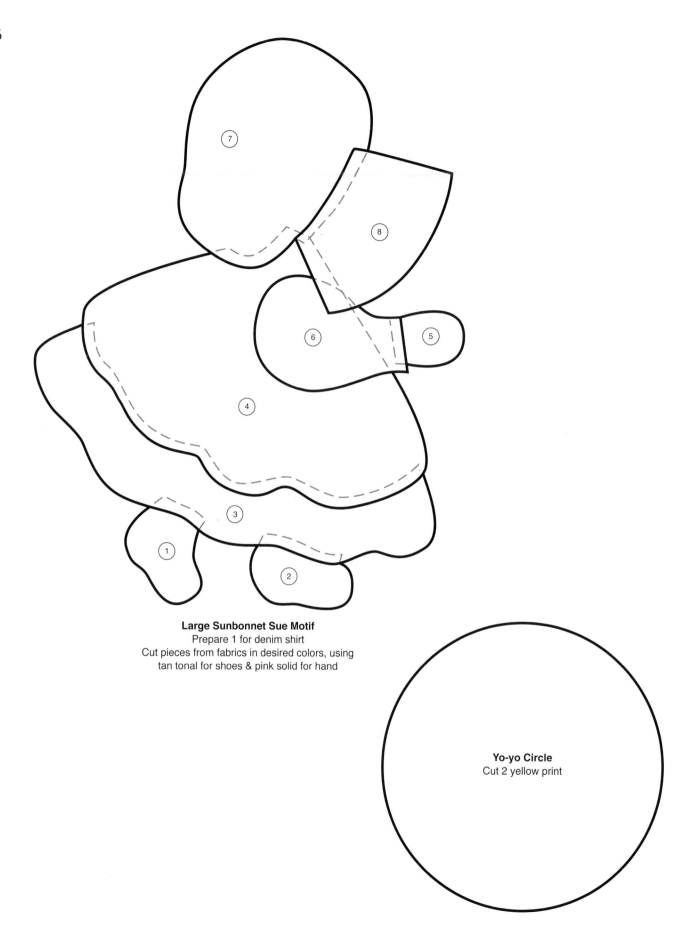

Large Sunbonnet Sue Motif
Prepare 1 for denim shirt
Cut pieces from fabrics in desired colors, using
tan tonal for shoes & pink solid for hand

Yo-yo Circle
Cut 2 yellow print

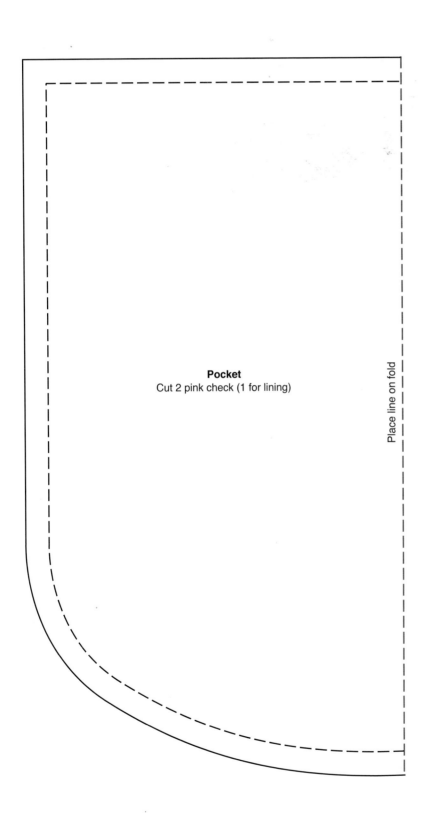

Pocket
Cut 2 pink check (1 for lining)

Place line on fold

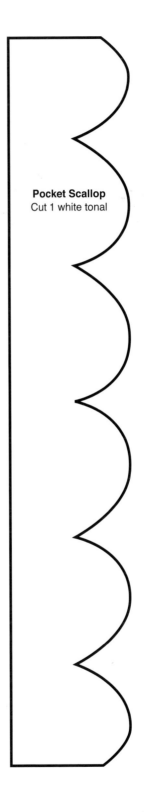

Pocket Scallop
Cut 1 white tonal

House of White Birches, Berne, Indiana 46711 Clotilde.com

Kitchen Collection

Sunbonnet Sue and Overall Bill love to help in the kitchen with pretty yet practical kitchen essentials. The apron, towels and pot holders are must-haves for any home!

Project Note
Fabrics used in the projects in the kitchen collection are 1930s reproduction prints.

Project Specifications
Skill Level: Beginner
Apron Size: One size fits most
Pot Holder Size: 8" x 8"
Block Size: 8" x 8"
Number of Blocks: 4

Materials
- Scraps black tonal and pink solid
- 1 fat eighth each white, pink and green prints
- Fat eighth teal floral
- Fat eighth yellow mottled
- ⅜ yard white tonal
- 1 yard white geometric print
- 1 yard lavender print
- (2) 9" x 9" squares heat-resistant batting
- Black and white all-purpose thread
- 1 yard 18"-wide fusible web
- Appliqué pressing sheet (optional)
- 3 cotton dish towels
- Basic sewing tools and supplies

Cutting Instructions for Set
1. Cut one 8½" by fabric width strip white tonal; subcut strip into four 8½" A squares.

2. Cut one 11½" by fabric width strip lavender print; subcut strip into one 12½" apron bib lining rectangle, one 4½" F strip, one 10½" E rectangle, one 8½" pocket lining rectangle and two 2½" C strips as shown in Figure 1.

3. Cut one 18½" by fabric width strip lavender print; subcut strip into one 23½" apron lining piece, two 6½" x 14½" G strips and two 2" x 8½" B strips, again referring to Figure 1.

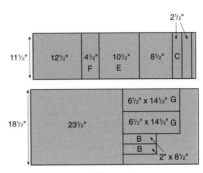

Figure 1

4. Cut two 2½" by fabric width strips white geometric print; subcut strips into two 23½" H strips and two 2" x 8½" D strips.

5. Cut three 2" by fabric width I strips white geometric print.

6. Cut one 8½" by fabric width strip white geometric print; subcut strip into two 8½" pot-holder backing squares.

7. Cut two 2¼" by fabric width strips white geometric print for binding.

8. Trace individual appliqué shapes as directed for number to cut onto the paper side of the fusible web; cut out shapes, leaving a ½" margin around each one.

9. Fuse shapes to the wrong side of fabrics as directed on patterns for color and number to cut; cut out shapes on traced lines. Remove paper backing.

Completing the Appliqué
1. Fold and crease two A squares on one diagonal to mark the center.

2. Center and fuse one Overall Bill motif with pieces in numerical order on the diagonal crease of one A square for the pot holder. ***Note:*** *Using an appliqué pressing sheet to fuse the motif together before fusing to A helps make this process more accurate.*

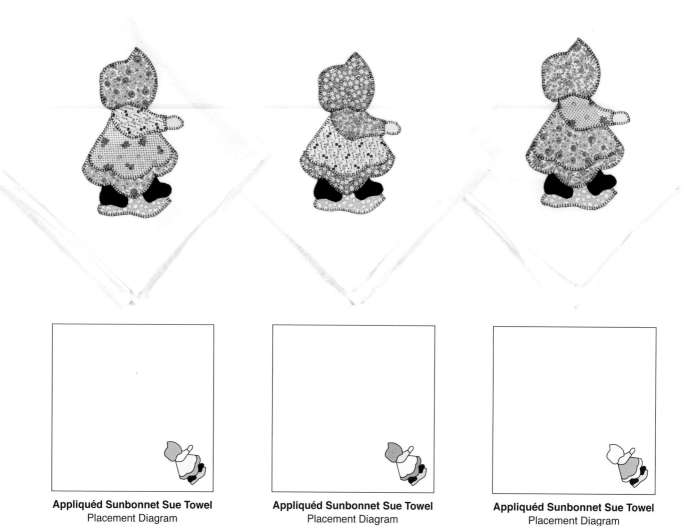

Appliquéd Sunbonnet Sue Towel
Placement Diagram
Size Varies

Appliquéd Sunbonnet Sue Towel
Placement Diagram
Size Varies

Appliquéd Sunbonnet Sue Towel
Placement Diagram
Size Varies

3. Repeat step 2 with a Sunbonnet Sue motif for a second pot holder.

4. Repeat steps 1 and 2 with the towels, centering one Sunbonnet Sue motif 3" from corner and 2" in from each side of each towel as shown in Figure 2.

Figure 2

5. Fold and crease the remaining A squares to mark the vertical and horizontal centerlines. Center and fuse one Overall Bill motif in numerical order on one A square and a Sunbonnet Sue motif on the other square for the apron.

6. Using black thread and a machine blanket stitch, stitch around each fused shape.

Completing the Pot Holders

1. Sandwich one 9" x 9" square heat-resistant batting between one appliquéd Overall Bill A square and one pot-holder backing square; pin or baste layers together to hold.

2. Quilt as desired by hand or machine; remove pins or basting.

3. Trim batting and backing edges even with the pot-holder tops.

4. Join the two binding strips on short ends with diagonal seams to make one long strip as shown in Figure 3; trim seams to ¼" and press open.

Figure 3

5. Fold the strip in half along length with wrong sides together; press.

6. With raw edges even, pin the binding strip to the right side of one pot holder; stitch all around, mitering corners and overlapping at the beginning and end. Trim excess binding.

7. Turn binding to the back side; hand-stitch in place.

8. Cut a 5" length from the remaining end of the trimmed binding strip.

9. Unfold the strip and fold again along length with right sides together; stitch along long raw edge as shown in Figure 4.

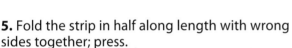

Figure 4

10. Turn the stitched tube right side out and press flat with seam on the side; topstitch close to each long edge.

11. Fold ⅜" at each end of the strip to the wrong side then fold the strip in half with the folded ends between to make a loop as shown in Figure 5.

Figure 5

12. Hand-stitch ends of loop in place on one corner of the pot holder to finish.

13. Repeat steps 1–12 to complete the Sunbonnet Sue pot holder.

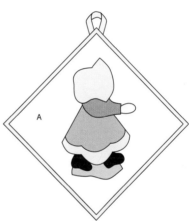

Sunbonnet Sue Pot Holder
Placement Diagram
8" x 8"

Overall Bill Pot Holder
Placement Diagram
8" x 8"

Completing the Apron

1. Sew a B strip to opposite sides and C strips to the top and bottom of the Sunbonnet Sue A square as shown in Figure 6; press seams toward B and C strips.

Figure 6

2. Place the 11½" x 12½" lining rectangle right sides together with the bordered Sunbonnet Sue block; stitch three sides, leaving the bottom edge open.

3. Turn right side out; press edges flat to complete the bib top.

4. Sew D strips to opposite sides of the Overall Bill A square as shown in Figure 7; press seams toward D strips.

Figure 7

5. Place the 8½" x 11½" lining rectangle right sides together with the bordered Overall Bill square; stitch the top edge.

6. Turn right side out; press edge flat to complete the pocket panel.

7. Place the pocket panel right side up on the right side of E aligning side and bottom raw edges as shown in Figure 8; machine-baste to hold together.

Figure 8

8. Sew the F strip to the bottom and a G rectangle to each side of the pocket panel as shown in Figure 9; press seams toward F and G.

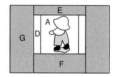

Figure 9

9. Sew an H strip to the top and bottom of the pocket panel to complete the apron skirt; press seams toward H strips.

10. Fold and crease the bib unit to mark the bottom center and the skirt unit to mark the top center.

11. With right sides together and matching creased lines, sew the bib unit to the skirt unit; press seam toward the H strip on the skirt unit.

12. Fold each I strip in half with right sides together to make three 1" x 21" strips; sew along the long raw edges of each strip to make three 21"-long tubes for neck and apron ties.

13. Turn each tube right side out; press edges flat. Turn in the raw ends of one strip ¼" and press to make the neck tie.

14. Pin the ends of the neck tie to the wrong side of the top of the bib at each corner; machine-stitch in place to hold.

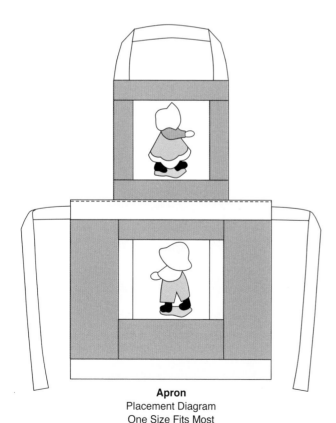

Apron
Placement Diagram
One Size Fits Most

15. Pin the raw end of each of the remaining I strips to the bottom of the top H strip as shown in Figure 10.

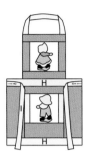

Figure 10

16. Pin the apron skirt lining right sides together with the apron skirt; trim edges even with the apron skirt if necessary. Stitch around sides and across bottom, leaving the top edge open. Turn right side out; press edges flat.

17. Turn under the raw edge of the top edge of the lining; press.

18. Topstitch the folded edge of the lining to cover the seam between the bib and the skirt as shown in Figure 11 to finish the apron. ❖

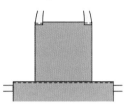

Figure 11

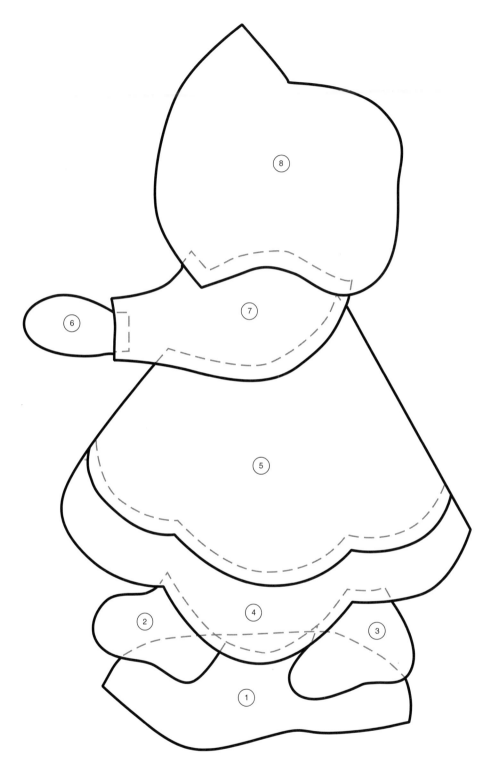

Sunbonnet Sue Motif
Prepare 1 each for pot holder & apron & 3 for towels
Cut pieces from fabrics in desired colors, using black
mottled for shoes & pink solid for hand

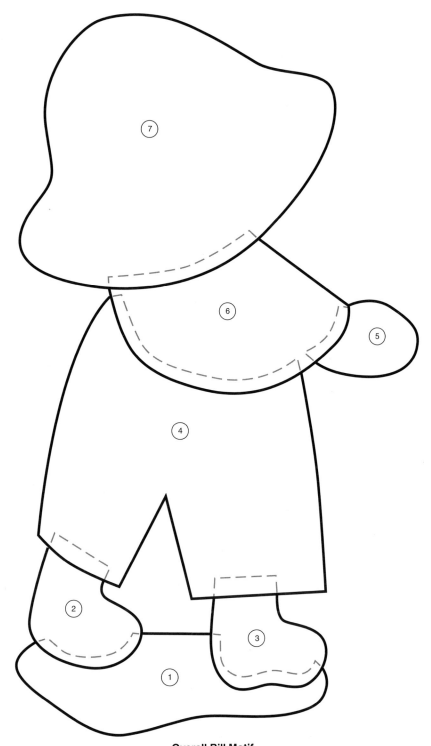

Overall Bill Motif
Prepare 1 each for pot holder & apron
Cut pieces from fabrics in desired colors, using black
mottled for shoes & pink solid for hand

House of White Birches, Berne, Indiana 46711   Clotilde.com

4

13

23

28

39

Metric Conversion Charts

Metric Conversions

Canada/U.S. Measurement			Multiplied by		Metric Measurement
yards	x	.9144	=		metres (m)
yards	x	91.44	=		centimetres (cm)
inches	x	2.54	=		centimetres (cm)
inches	x	25.40	=		millimetres (mm)
inches	x	.0254	=		metres (m)

Canada/U.S. Measurement			Multiplied by		Metric Measurement
centimetres	x	.3937	=		inches
metres	x	1.0936	=		yards

Standard Equivalents

Canada/U.S. Measurement				Metric Measurement
⅛ inch	=	3.20 mm	=	0.32 cm
¼ inch	=	6.35 mm	=	0.635 cm
⅜ inch	=	9.50 mm	=	0.95 cm
½ inch	=	12.70 mm	=	1.27 cm
⅝ inch	=	15.90 mm	=	1.59 cm
¾ inch	=	19.10 mm	=	1.91 cm
⅞ inch	=	22.20 mm	=	2.22 cm
1 inch	=	25.40 mm	=	2.54 cm
⅛ yard	=	11.43 cm	=	0.11 m
¼ yard	=	22.86 cm	=	0.23 m
⅜ yard	=	34.29 cm	=	0.34 m
½ yard	=	45.72 cm	=	0.46 m
⅝ yard	=	57.15 cm	=	0.57 m
¾ yard	=	68.58 cm	=	0.69 m
⅞ yard	=	80.00 cm	=	0.80 m
1 yard	=	91.44 cm	=	0.91 m
1⅛ yards	=	102.87 cm	=	1.03 m
1¼ yards	=	114.30 cm	=	1.14 m

Canada/U.S. Measurement		Metric Measurement		Metric Measurement
1⅜ yards	=	125.73 cm	=	1.26 m
1½ yards	=	137.16 cm	=	1.37 m
1⅝ yards	=	148.59 cm	=	1.49 m
1¾ yards	=	160.02 cm	=	1.60 m
1⅞ yards	=	171.44 cm	=	1.71 m
2 yards	=	182.88 cm	=	1.83 m
2⅛ yards	=	194.31 cm	=	1.94 m
2¼ yards	=	205.74 cm	=	2.06 m
2⅜ yards	=	217.17 cm	=	2.17 m
2½ yards	=	228.60 cm	=	2.29 m
2⅝ yards	=	240.03 cm	=	2.40 m
2¾ yards	=	251.46 cm	=	2.51 m
2⅞ yards	=	262.88 cm	=	2.63 m
3 yards	=	274.32 cm	=	2.74 m
3⅛ yards	=	285.75 cm	=	2.86 m
3¼ yards	=	297.18 cm	=	2.97 m
3⅜ yards	=	308.61 cm	=	3.09 m
3½ yards	=	320.04 cm	=	3.20 m
3⅝ yards	=	331.47 cm	=	3.31 m
3¾ yards	=	342.90 cm	=	3.43 m
3⅞ yards	=	354.32 cm	=	3.54 m
4 yards	=	365.76 cm	=	3.66 m
4⅛ yards	=	377.19 cm	=	3.77 m
4¼ yards	=	388.62 cm	=	3.89 m
4⅜ yards	=	400.05 cm	=	4.00 m
4½ yards	=	411.48 cm	=	4.11 m
4⅝ yards	=	422.91 cm	=	4.23 m
4¾ yards	=	434.34 cm	=	4.34 m
4⅞ yards	=	445.76 cm	=	4.46 m
5 yards	=	457.20 cm	=	4.57 m

E-mail: Customer_Service@whitebirches.com

HOUSE of WHITE BIRCHES
PUBLISHERS SINCE 1947

Sunbonnet Sue Once Upon a Posy is published by DRG, 306 East Parr Road, Berne, IN 46711, telephone (260) 589-4000. Printed in USA. Copyright © 2010 DRG. All rights reserved. This publication may not be reproduced in part or in whole without written permission from the publisher.

RETAIL STORES: If you would like to carry this pattern book or any other DRG publications, call the Wholesale Department at Annie's Attic to set up a direct account: (903) 636-4303. Also, request a complete listing of publications available from DRG.

Every effort has been made to ensure that the instructions in this pattern book are complete and accurate. We cannot, however, take responsibility for human error, typographical mistakes or variations in individual work.

STAFF

Editor: Jeanne Stauffer
Editorial Assistant: Stephanie Timm
Technical Editor: Sandra Hatch
Technical Artist: Connie Rand
Copy Supervisor: Michelle Beck
Copy Editors: Angie Buckles, Emily Carter, Amanda Scheerer
Production Artist Supervisor: Erin Augsburger

Graphic Artists: Glenda Chamberlain, Edith Teegarden
Art Director: Brad Snow
Assistant Art Director: Nick Pierce
Photography Supervisor: Tammy Christian
Photography: Matthew Owen
Photo Stylists: Tammy Liechty, Tammy Steiner

ISBN: 978-1-59217-310-5

1 2 3 4 5 6 7 8 9